Free to Dance

God's Purpose for the Dance

by Eileen Schultz

Foreword by Dr. Bill Hamon

Cover Design by Kendall Shell

Available through:

Preparing The Way Ministries
Steve & Eileen Schultz, P.O. Box 1711,
Santa Rosa Beach, Florida 32459 USA

Distributed in the U.S.A. by
Christian International Ministries
P.O. Box 9000
Santa Rosa Beach, FL 32459 U.S.A.

Copyright 1997

Eileen Schultz, P.O. Box 1711, Santa Rosa Beach, Fl 32459 U.S.A.

OTHER BOOKS BY STEVE SCHULTZ
Radical Warriors Require Radical Training
Restoration of the Modern Day Prophet
Mentoring & Fathering

All rights reserved. No part of this book may be reproduced in any form without permission in writing from the author.

Printed in U.S.A.

ISBN 0-9624461-8-1

Unless otherwise noted, all Scriptures are taken from the King James Version of the Bible.

TABLE OF CONTENTS

CHAPTER   PAGE

Dedication   v
FOREWORD   vii
Introduction   ix

1 The Foundation and Restoration
   of Dance   1

2 God's Purposes for Dance   15

3 Three Types of Dance   33

4 Obstacles To Overcome   51

5 Performance Vs Ministry   75

6 Dynamics of Team Ministry   87

7 Dancing With Excellence   111

   References and Suggested Reading   118

DEDICATION

*I would like to dedicate this book
to my immediate family
(Steve, Aaron and Nathan)
and to my mom, Mitzi Eagles.
They have been a constant source of
encouragement in my quest
to be Free To Dance!*

FOREWORD
By
DR. BILL HAMON

Eileen Schultz has done an outstanding job of showing the biblical validity of worship and praise to God through the expression of dance. There are hundreds of scriptures in the Bible exhorting saints to worship God with the bodily expressions of shouting, singing, raising the arms, clapping our hands, and dancing with our feet. God had many of the prophets to act out their prophecies by silent pantomime and some dance movements. King David who worshiped before the Lord by dancing with all his might is stated in the Bible as a man after God's own heart. No where in scripture does it ever limit anyone in their creative praise to worship God. The only requirements are that it be done with all of our heart as unto the Lord. It is best accepted by people when it is done in an humble attitude, holy character, modest clothing, and an excellent performance.

Eileen gives many guidelines for one developing their personal ability as an individual praise dancer. Many directives are given for properly developing a dance team that can work together with one another and the pastor. Wise counsel is presented to enable a praise dance leader to develop a dance team that can bless the church and glorify God.

I highly recommend this book to those who are interested in knowing more about praising God in the dance and choreographed dancing within the church.

Dr. Bill Hamon
CEO and Bishop of Christian International Ministries Network
Author of: "The Eternal Church"
"Prophets-1 Personal Prophecy"
"Prophets-2 The Prophetic Movement"
"Prophets-3 Pitfalls and Principles"
"Fulfilling Your Personal Prophecy"
"Prophetic Destiny and the Apostolic Reformation"
"Apostles-Prophets and the Coming Moves of God"

INTRODUCTION

This book was not only written for those that feel called to a dance team ministry, but for anyone who desires to worship God in the dance. It was birthed out of a great need that I recognized in regards to understanding the purpose of dance and its role in today's Church. I, possibly like you, have always had a desire to express myself through dance and yet for years saw no expression or outlet for dance in the Christian world.

Thank God we are living in a time of the restoration of all things (Acts 3:21-22) and the Lord is restoring to the church all the expressions of Davidic worship, including the praise dance. Because of the traditions of men and the fear of the extreme, Satan was able to steal and pervert the art of dance from God's people. We must realize that the dance originated with God and was created by Him for His purposes.

The title, *Free To Dance*, carries with it the flavor of my own need for the truth and the personal struggles of being free to express myself through dance in the Church. Before being saved, I had a great desire to dance and expressed myself through dance in the worldly environment. But even then, it never fulfilled me.

After my salvation experience in 1982, I totally died to my desire to dance because I thought there was no place for it in Christianity. In 1984 while visiting a church, I received my first prophetic word from Dr. Bill Hamon who was the guest speaker. A portion of the prophetic word spoke to my future ministry and potential. It stated: *"And the Lord says, you're gonna be a praiser and a worshiper and a **dancer** before Me and you have been loosed from the things of this world. You're going to be **trained and equipped** and I have put the worship of the Lord in you and you are going to have a prophetic anointing upon you like Debra of old and you are going to see the flow of God within your spirit. I loose you and call you forth this night and I am going to start you in training, saith the Lord thy God."*

At this particular time in my life, the only type of dancing I had seen was the expression of praise dance during the praise & worship time, commonly known as the "Holy Hop." I had never been exposed to any other forms of dance in the church setting and I also had never been taught the validity and value of personal prophecy. Therefore, when I received this prophetic word I didn't pursue the dance in that season of my life.

It was not until 1987 when I attended my first Christian International conference, that I actually saw dance in a broader dimension. During the conference, Mary Webster (who is now a good friend of mine) ministered an interpretive dance special. At that time I began to realize that dance was not limited to congregational worship. While watching Mary, a new spark of desire to dance began to ignite within my spirit. I saw that Mary had a freedom to minister before God and the people that I did not have and that I greatly desired.

From 1987 until 1990, I was continually exposed to dance through several CI seminars and through several churches in the Atlanta, Geogia area. It was during this period that God began to nurture my desire to worship Him through the expression of dance. I was continually confronted with an internal conflict of a desire to dance before the Lord, yet bound by a fear of man and an inability to express my passion to God through dance. I was emotionally handicapped.

At the end of 1990, we moved to Santa Rosa Beach, Florida to become a part of Christian International Ministries. In 1991, I finally worked up the courage to become a part of CI's dance team. From that time until now, God has been progressively delivering me from the fear of man, sharpening my skills, and unlocking the passion in my heart for Him that for so many years was imprisoned. Anointed C.I. dance instructors such as Donetta Barret, Sharon Potter, Rodney Purvis and Yvonne Williams of Arts Triumphant have been instrumental in helping me to grow through these processes. I also thank God for Bishop and Mom Hamon and Pastors Tom and Jane Hamon for embracing the ministry art of dance and for their personal encouragement in my calling and ministry.

My desire for you is that while reading this book, the truths and practical insights presented will encourage you to experience a greater personal freedom in dance. That they would also assist you in finding your identity as a worshipper and give you greater practical insights to many different aspects of dance such as overcoming obstacles, establishing a dance team, forms of dance, choreography, etc.

My prayers is that this book will help clarify a subject which has been controversial and will hopefully inspire you to further insights and exploration.

In His Service,

Eileen Schultz

CHAPTER ONE

THE FOUNDATION AND RESTORATION OF DANCE

When one talks about the dance, the common response from most people is, "Dancing in the Church? Is that allowed?" Since the Bible is the foundation for all that Christians believe and all that they do, we will begin our journey by investigating praise dance from a scriptural perspective.

IS DANCE IN THE BIBLE?

Numerous scriptures throughout the Bible

Free To Dance

speak of the reality of dance as a form of worship. We are commanded by scripture to love the Lord God with all our heart, soul, mind and **strength**. (Mark 12:30). Strength speaks of the physical. Does that mean we should run an Olympic marathon or bench press 300 pounds a day in the name of the Lord? Thank God He doesn't require that of us! (Ha! Ha!) Obviously 'strength' speaks of the use of our body towards God as an instrument of worship. David danced before the Lord with all his might! (2 Sam 6:14)

Dancing allows the believer another realm to express our worship besides such gestures as bowing, kneeling, clapping, raising of hands . . . . realizing that the expression of worship through dance utilizes a **combination of many physical gestures** of worship found in scripture.

Numerous scriptures speak of the dance. The following scriptures are some of the most popular:

The Foundation & Restoration of Dance

*"A time to weep, and a time to laugh; and a time to mourn, and a time to **dance**;"* Ec. 3:4

*"Praise him with the timbrel and **dance**:"* Psalm 150:4

*"Let them praise his name in the **dance**: let them sing praises unto him with the timbrel and harp."* Psalm 149:3

*Thou hast turned for me my mourning into **dancing**:"* Psalm 30:11

There are numerous Hebrew words which speak of dancing and rejoicing before the Lord. As an example, the Hebrew word **gul** or **gil** (S.C. 1523) means to spin around (under the influence of any violent emotion); to rejoice; be glad; to go in a circle. It is found in numerous places such as Ps. 2:11; 9:14; 13:4-5; 14:7; 16:9; 21:11; 31:7; 32:11; 35:9; etc.

Another is the Hebrew word **chul** or **chil**

Free To Dance

which means to twist or whirl (in a circular manner); to dance; to turn around; to dance in a circle. This word is used in places such as Duet. 2:25; Judges. 21:21-23; Job 15:50; Ps. 29:9; Is. 13:8; 23:4; 26:17-18; 54:1; 66:7-9; Jer. 4:19, etc.

Other words which relate to dance are words such as **machol** (which means a dance or dancing chorus) Ps. 30:11, 149:3, 150:4, Jer. 31:4,13, Lam. 5:15; **macholah** (S.C. 4246) (which means a round dance or company of dancer) Ex. 15:20, 32:19, Judg. 11:34, 21:21, 1 Sam. 18:6, 21:11, 29:5, 1 Kings 19:6; **karar** (which means to dance; to move in a circle) 2 Sam. 6:14; **rekad** (which means to stamp, to spring about) 1 Chron. 15:29, Job 21:11, Ps. 29:6, 114:4 & 6, Ecc. 3:4, Is. 13:21, Joel 2:5, Nahum 3:2; **dalag** (which means to spring or leap) 2 Sam. 22:30, Ps. 18:29, Is. 35:6, Song of Sol. 2:8, Zeph. 1:9; and **pazez** (which means to leap, to bound, be light, agile) Gen. 49:24, 2 Sam. 6:16.

The Foundation & Restoration of Dance

Overall their are eleven terms to describe the act of dance in the Old Testament and three terms used in the New Testament. The New Testament terms are: **1) agalliao** (S.C. 21) which means to jump for joy and is translated "exult," " be exceeding glad, " "with exceeding joy," "rejoice greatly" (Luke 1:14, 44, 47; 10:21; Matthew 5:12; John 5:35; 8:56; Acts 2:26, 46; 16:34; 1 Peter 1:6,8; Revelation 19:7) **2) skirtao** (S.C. 4640) which means to jump, move, leap for joy or to skip and is used in Luke 1:41, 44; 6:23 **3) hallomai** (S.C. 242) which means to jump, leap, spring up as used in John 4:14; Acts 3:8; 14:10 - The lame man went walking and leaping and praising God into the Temple with Peter and John..

SCRIPTURAL EXAMPLES OF DANCING

Dancing before the Lord can be found in such places as:

- Miriam danced at the Red Sea Ex.

16:20
- Children of Israel danced at David's defeat of the Philistine. 1 Sam. 18:6
- David danced while bringing the ark into the city of David. 2 Sam. 6:16

Dancing as an expression of worship, joy and victory can be found in such places as:

- The children of Israel danced before the golden calf. Ex. 32:19
- David's enemies danced at their victory and their obtaining of spoils 1 Sam. 30:16
- Pagans used dance as a means of honoring their Gods. 1 Kings 18:26

THE RESTORATION OF THE DANCE

Now that we see that dancing is throughout the Bible and is a scriptural form of worship, let us take a brief look at the history of the dance in the life of the children of Israel (O.T.) and in the Church (N.T.).

The Foundation & Restoration of Dance

Dancing was an essential part of Jewish life in Bible times. Dances were exhibited on both secular and sacred occasions. Some of these occasions are:

- ☞ As a custom at weddings - On some occasions young ladies, dressed in their best clothing, danced in a bride-choosing ceremony (Judges 21). Marriage processions involved dancing with timbrels and other musical instruments (Ps. 45:14-15). Dances were performed in honor of the bride (Song of Sol. 6:13).
- ☞ Some dances were performed for the sheer entertainment of guests. Salome danced before the princes and politicians gathered to celebrate her father's birthday (Matt. 14:6; Mark 6:22).
- ☞ Children played games of "dance" (Job 21:11).
- ☞ Dances also celebrated military victories. Miriam and the other Israelite

Free To Dance

women sang and danced in celebration of the victory at the Red Sea (Ex. 15:20-21). Jephthah's daughter danced before her victorious father (Judges 11:34). The Israelite women danced when David returned from having defeated the Philistines (1 Sam 18:6).

☞ Remember, at the return of the prodigal son, it was a cause for celebration and dancing (Luke 15:25).

☞ The most often occasion for dancing was at religious celebrations. As an example, when David brought the ark into Jerusalem (2 Sam. 6:14,16; 1 Chron. 15:29). The psalmist exhorted others to praise God with music and dancing (Ps. 149:3; 150:4). Even pagans used the dance as a means of honoring and worshiping their gods. 1 Kings 18:26.

As we can see, dancing was truly an acceptable practice in the life of the children of Israel.

The Foundation & Restoration of Dance

One of the greatest displays of the dance, in its sacred form, is found in the Old Testament in the Tabernacle of David. After David set up the Tabernacle of David and instituted worship before God's ark on a twenty four hour a day basis (I Ch. 16:4-6,37-40; 25) the worship teams would praise God continually (Heb. 13:15) with music, singing, clapping, shouting, bowing and **dancing**. (It is interesting to note that in I Chronicles 15 that wherever the word "played" is used, it is the Hebrew word "sachaq" which communicates the idea of dancing to the sound of music.) Even in the midst of O.T. law, God allowed David (the man after God's own heart) to establish a pattern of worship that still carries over to the New Testament. (For further study of the Tabernacle of David and its spiritual restoration, please see recommended reading list for books specializing in this subject.)

If dancing was so prevalent in the Hebrew lifestyle, then why haven't we seen a greater expression and demonstration of dance throughout Church history? Unfortunately with the decline of Christianity during the Dark Ages (500-1500 A.D.), many truths and practices were lost or polluted by worldly influence. Since the Reformation, we have witnessed the Spirit of the Lord progressively restoring scriptural truth to the Church. (I strongly suggest that you read *The Eternal Church* by Dr. Bill Hamon for greater understanding on the different restoration movements and the truths restored during these movements.) The restoration of truth not only applies to areas such as salvation, healing, deliverance, holiness, the Holy Spirit, etc., but it also applies to progressively restoring truth about praise and worship.

Today, we are living in a time of the restoration of the arts (drama, mime, dance, etc.) to the Church. David's Tabernacle is literally being "spiritually restored" (Amos 9:11) and we are learning to worship God in spirit and in truth (John 4:24).

The Foundation & Restoration of Dance

EXTREMES AND COUNTERFEITS

As with any restoration of truth, there are extremes and counterfeits. The dance is no exception. One of the devil's greatest deceptions is to pervert what God has given to the Church and to convince Christians that what God calls sanctified, we sometimes call worldly.

We must remember that for every truth, there is always a counterfeit. We see this principle demonstrated in such things as counterfeit money. Counterfeit money is illegal in our country yet thousands of illegal dollars are produced every year. These counterfeits look exactly like real dollars to the average person, yet a trained professional can spot the difference immediately.

Another example is the present day restoration of the prophetic ministry. As God is restoring prophets to the Church, Satan is deceiving thousands every year through the psychic

Free To Dance

realm. Both appear to be very similar but are motivated by different spirits. It is only as one handles and/or experiences the real that the counterfeit becomes evident.

Dancing is very similar in that it is being restored to the Church in its fulness as an expression of worship and warfare. We must remember that every time God restores a truth to the Church, most of the existing "church people" are fearful, critical and doubtful of the validity of that particular truth. Today, because of 1) worldly association, 2) pre-conceived mind-sets, and 3) lack of understanding of the restoration of the Tabernacle of David, many Christians have either ignored or chosen to suppress dance in all its Godly forms as a valid expression of worship.

Thank God that we are living in an exciting season of restoration and we are seeing God convert what the devil has tried to misuse and pervert. Around the world, praise dance is

The Foundation & Restoration of Dance

once again becoming a viable and visible part of the Christian Church. Let us go on to the next chapter where we will investigate some of the purposes for the dance.

Free To Dance

CHAPTER TWO

GOD'S PURPOSES FOR DANCE

There are number of purposes for the dance as an expression of praise to God. Before we investigate these, please allow me to list a few basic reasons why we should praise the Lord in all the forms and expressions of worship which He has revealed through scripture.

WHY WE PRAISE GOD

There are a number of reasons why we praise the Lord:

#1) We praise God because we are

Free To Dance

commanded to do so! Psalm 150:1 states, "Praise ye the Lord" and (over 38 times we are commanded to "praise ye the Lord.") Not that God needs our praise, as He is the All Sufficient One and doesn't have need of anything! We praise God because we are the beneficiaries of praise. Praise is an avenue to come into proper relationship with Him.

#2) We praise God because there is power in praise. Praise is a spiritual weapon of warfare which can bring victory, power, deliverance, blessing and break-through. (2 Chron. 20; Psalm 8:2 and many others.)

#3) We praise Him because we were instruments created by Him to praise Him! (1 Peter 2:9; Is. 43:21; Eph. 1:11)

#4) We also praise Him because He is worthy of our praises. (Psalm 48:1; Rev. 4:11)

#5) We praise Him because He is enthroned in our praises. (Psalm 22:3) In other words, God

God's Purposes For Dance

responds and inhabits our praises.

This is not an all-inclusive list of the reasons why we praise the Lord but I believe complete enough to show that each Christian has a responsibility to worship the Lord.

Now, I am sure you are asking, "What further purposes could dance have as an expression of worship?" Glad you asked! Let's look at six reasons (purposes) God created dance. (Again, let me emphasize that dance is many times a combination of the other expressive forms of worship such as leaping, twirling, clapping hands, waving hands, kneeling, etc.)

PURPOSE #1&2 - GOD CREATED DANCE AS A MEANS TO *COMMUNICATE* AND *DEMONSTRATE*

From the beginning, God showed His creativity and His desire to communicate. He fashioned the earth and man and then immediately began to communicate with His

Free To Dance

creation.

From that time until now, God is still desiring to create and communicate. We know He didn't stop talking and creating in the Garden of Eden. Even today God's creative nature flows through us in such areas as artwork and inventions. Some of us may not feel very gifted in this creative area, but let me encourage you by saying that we are **all creative** to one degree or another because we are made in His image and we have been given His ability to create. Therefore I believe we can tap into this creative ability in different ways and on different levels.

Not only is God still creating, but He is still communicating, As we know God communicates in various means and ways. Such as through the Bible, through angelic visitation, through the inward witness, through the five-fold ministry (Eph. 4:11), through dreams, through His people and even through nature. Romans 1:20 states, "Through the

God's Purposes For Dance

creation of the world, God's invisible qualities - His eternal power and divine nature have been clearly **seen** and understood." His creation is truly a visible demonstration of His desire to communicate and an example of one of His methods of communicating.

We have all heard the phrase that a picture paints a thousands words. Visual communication is a very powerful and stimulating means to convey a message. In the Old Testament times the basis of the people's relationship with the Lord was by **sight** - they **saw** the cloud and fire. In Hosea 12:10, Hosea reveals this when he writes, "I have spoken to you by the prophets and I have multiplied visions for you and have appealed to you through parables **acted out by the prophets**." Other examples are:

- ♦ Isaiah was commanded by God to strip and walk naked for three years as a sign and forewarning to the children of Israel.

- God gave Moses the pattern of the Tabernacle of Moses as a visual and tangible evidence of the law. Today, His tabernacle is still speaking to the church through types and shadows.

In the New Testament, Jesus understood the value and strength of pictures as He spoke numerous times in parabolic form. Parables are messages which give us a mental (visual) image which make a lasting impression and help us to retain what has been communicated. Not only did Jesus communicate verbally but others did also such as:

- Agabus the prophet communicated a prophetic message in Acts. In Acts 21: 10 & 11, Prophet Agabus entered Caesarea from Judea to deliver a message to the Apostle Paul. His message is not only delivered verbally but he physically demonstrates the prophetic message by removing Paul's belt and tying Paul's hands.

Numerous studies have shown that most communication is given in a non-verbal format. These studies have revealed that between 70 and 80% of communication can be non-verbal. While doing these studies, they discovered that non-verbal communication can be divided into several different categories. Non-verbal communication includes:

✻ **Kinesics** - This is basically concerned with body movements - head, eyes, shoulders, neck, legs, arms, fingers, hands and gestures.

✻ **Appearance** - This is concerned with the physical appearance, clothing and adornments.

✻ **Silence** - If we think about it, silence can be as communicative as speaking. We have all heard of the stony stare - no words but lots of meaning - and mostly not very positive.

✻ **Paralinguistics** - This is concerned with tone and sounds. These are the sounds we make that are not actually words. Sounds like "Umm!" and "Umph!".

Free To Dance

It is also interesting to note *that the majority of non-verbal communication is found under the category of "kinesics."* Yes, we many times say more with our bodies than we do with our words. Have you ever noticed how many people use their hands while talking and that their gestures often times communicate more than their words. In these studies a fact is brought out that some cultures tend to use body language more frequently than others.

I myself, coming from a Jewish background, have inherited the gift of "hand gab!" I recently had a conversation with a friend where I was telling him a story. At the finish of the story, he grabbed both of my hands, restricting them and replied, "Now, tell that story again!" All I could do was laugh knowing that I could never have conversation without **lots** of gesturing.

Another short illustration of non-verbal communication can even be found in the animal kingdom. I always know when my

God's Purposes For Dance

four pound tea-cup poodle, Jasmine, has done something wrong. She seems to loose 2" of length from her 4" legs as she cowers and scoots around the house in a guilt ridden posture.

From all the above, we can see how God uses the dance as an unspoken language to demonstrates and communicate. A dancer's movements (body language) become that visual art form which communicates an individual message or enhances other modes of communication. Enhancing other modes of communication can be seen when dance is combined with a song. Not only is the message heard, but the message is also **seen, which as a result creates a greater impact**. Dance truly adds a visual dimension of communication to an anointed song. In the next chapter I will cover three different categories of dance that will explain how we communicate to God and how He communicates to us through dance.

Free To Dance

I would like to share with you a quote given by Doris Humphrey in 1937 that beautifully relates to this aspect of communication and dance:

> *"The dancer believes that his art has something to say which can not be expressed in words or in any other way than by dancing....there are times when the simple dignity of movement can fulfill the function of a volume of words. There are movements which impinge upon the nerves with a strength that is incomparable, for movement has power to stir the senses and emotions, unique in itself. This is the dancer's justification for being, and his reason for searching further for deeper aspects of his art."*

PURPOSE #3 & 4 - GOD CREATED DANCE AS A MEANS TO *MOTIVATE* AND *LIBERATE*

God's Purposes For Dance

Another purpose for dance is that it is motivational. As one dances, the nature of the dance can motivate in three different realms. Let's look at these three - **God** (heavenly), **others** (human) and **ourselves** (heart):

⏭ The first realm where dance motivates is in the **heavenly realm** (God). Psalm 22:3 states that "God inhabits the praises of his people." "Praises" in this particular scripture is the Hebrew word *halal* which means to make a show, to boast, to act clamorously foolish. As one dances before the Lord and makes an open show of their love and adoration for Him through physical expression, then the scripture promises us that **God is motivated to respond to our worship by inhabiting our praises**. Of course, we know that when God's presence arises in our worship, we can expect the manifestation of His power and glory in such ways as deliverance, healings, pulling down of strongholds, etc. Thank God we worship a living God who

Free To Dance

responds to our dances as opposed to the story of the prophets of Baal "who danced upon the altar from morning until noon saying, 'O Baal, hear and answer us!' But there was no voice, no one answered." (1 Kings 18:26 NIV)

▶ The second realm where dance motivates is in the **human realm** (others). As an individual or as team of dancers minister before the Lord, their dance can motivate in a number of different ways:

- In a congregational setting, dance has the ability to motivate and liberate others to enter in. As an example, when Miriam began to dance at the Red Sea (Ex. 16:20), the other women were motivated to join in and dance also. Most charismatic Christians have been in a congregational meeting where the spontaneity of a person dancing has "sparked" the entire congregation to worship in the dance.

God's Purposes For Dance

- In an evangelistic setting, dance can motivate the lost to open their hearts and liberate them to receive the gospel. Dance has the power to override human logic and go straight to the heart. The reason it does is that by its very nature it can stir the emotions, therefore opening the windows of the soul and penetrating the heart. Ministries such as Toymakers Dream, a non-verbal dance and drama team, have seen thousands come to the Lord through their presentation.

On the negative side, dance also is used by the enemy to motivate. In Matthew 14:6 the dancing of Herodius's daughter motivated Herod to murder John the Baptist.

⏭ The last realm where dance motivates and also liberates is in the **heart realm** (ourselves). It motivates us to set aside our inhibitions and liberates us to be free before

Free To Dance

God. Generally I have noticed that to the measure that people are free to dance is also a good measure of how spiritually free they are. We must remember that the body is an outward expression of the spirit man. If man chooses to yield to fear or pride, then the body responds through immobility. But when one chooses to humble themselves and dance as an act of their will, the movements of the dance release their passion and expressions to Him causing pride and other obstacles to crumble. It takes a humble heart to enter into this type of worship and it is a humble-open heart that God can reach in and touch.

1 Cor 15:46 relates that the spiritual didn't come first, but the natural. As we choose to express our praise through dance (natural), it releases and motivates within us the fruit of the spirit - love, joy, and peace, etc. (spiritual). I can remember a season in my life where God seemed distant and it was hard to enter in. It was as if I had a numb

Dancer = instruments of prophetic warfare allow God to take us to place of burnt sacrifice

God's Purposes For Dance

heart and "lead feet" and it was very difficult to dance. It was during this time that I would choose to dance sacrificially and as an act of my will. My spirit was willing but my flesh was weak (Matthew 26:41). In doing so, before long my dancing had motivated me into a place to where I could receive God's love and presence and liberate me from the enemies oppression.

There may be seasons and times in your life when you may feel bondage in certain areas and your joy has been lost. The children of Israel experienced the same thing when they were taken into Babylonian bondage and the **dance was lost**. Lamentations 5:15 says, "The joy of our heart is ceased, our dance is turned into mourning." When there was no dancing in Israel, it was a sign of mourning. Likewise, when a person is in spiritual bondage, their joy and dancing are lost. But praise God, He can turn our mourning into dancing!

During Worship (dance) give hearts to others
need to be clean to come into presence of God
vulnerable place where heart must be right
We minister what is in our heart

Free To Dance

PURPOSE #5 & 6 - GOD CREATED DANCE AS A MEANS TO *CELEBRATE* AND *COMMEMORATE*

Because dance is a form of communication, we can use the dance as an expression of celebration and thanksgiving for who He is, what He has done for us, and what He is yet to do for us. The word celebrate means to rejoice and act joyfully at a certain event or in remembrance of something special to us. The word commemorate means to honor something or someone or to preserve the memory of something. As an example dancing can be used to celebrate certain events such as spiritual breakthroughs and natural breakthroughs, both corporate and individual.

We can also dance to commemorate or honor something or someone. For example, in May of 1997, three of Evelyn Hamon's granddaughters dedicated a special dance presentation to honor her 60th birthday which deeply touched her heart. (How much more is

God's Purposes For Dance

God's heart touched when we dance before Him in honor for what He has done for us or who He is to us.)

The Bible clearly shows us a number of examples where dancing was the expression of celebration and commemoration:

☺ Exodus 15:20 - Miriam and the women in Israel danced and sang before the Lord with timbrels after the victory at the Red Sea. They danced out of great joy before the Lord for such deliverance. It was unto the Lord, not to man or mere display.

☺ Judges 11:34 - Jephthah's daughter came out to meet her father with timbrel and dances after the victory the Lord had given in the battle against the Ammonites.

☺ 1 Samuel 18:6 & 7; 21:11; 29:5 - The women of Israel sang and danced with tablets of joy and instruments of music after David had killed Goliath of Gath.

Free To Dance

☺ 2 Samuel 6:14-16 - David danced before the Lord at the coming of the ark on the day of dedication of the Tabernacle of David. (Same account found in 1 Chronicles 15:29.)

☺ Luke 15:25 - At the return of the prodigal son to the father's house, there was music and dancing.

Please allow me to encourage you that during your times of worship before the Lord, that you would personalize your dance to Him, remembering all the wonderful things He has done and is going to do for you!

Before we go on, let's again review the purposes of dance. God created dance as a means to:

1) COMMUNICATE & DEMONSTRATE
2) MOTIVATE & LIBERATE
3) CELEBRATE & COMMEMORATE

CHAPTER THREE

THREE TYPES OF DANCE

Now that we have briefly covered the history and purposes of dance, now let us explore three different and popular types of dance, realizing that these categories are not all inclusive. We will define these dances and explain their individual function and purpose.

In order to better understand the nature and function of each type of dance, please note that I will precede each dance description with

Free To Dance

a small diagram and explanation which will show the source of the communication and the object to which the communication is intended.

CHOREOGRAPHED DANCE

G O D

⬈

[dancers] ➡ | PEOPLE |

In a choreographed dance, the flow of communication is directed to God or may be directed to the people. [NOTE THAT THE DIAGRAM OF THE DANCERS REPRESENTS NOT ONLY A TEAM OF DANCERS BUT COULD **ALSO** BE A SOLO DANCER]

Three Types of Dancing

DEFINITION: Choreographed dance is the art of creating pre-arranged dance steps which are practiced before ministering. Choreographed dance can convey a message or an expression such as hope, joy, victory or celebration. Choreographed dancing can also be tailored to specific ministry such as evangelistic outreach. It can be comprised of many different styles, such as ballet, jazz, modern, etc.

PRACTICAL INSIGHTS: When one begins to develop and assemble a choreographed dance, here are a few insights which I trust will help:

❶ Make sure the lyrics of the song used are clearly heard and that the dancer(s) clearly understand the message to be conveyed.

❷ Make sure the music being used will relay a message for the church body and that it will edify, uplift, show the nature of God, glorify or tell a Bible truth.

❸ When choreographing, don't over interpret. Every single word doesn't necessarily need to be interpreted by a specific a movement. Like a Polaroid picture, allow the dance to slowly develop.

❹ Realize that there are various approaches to choreographing:
Hearing/Seeing - Some people see different movements in their minds eye while listening to the music.
Hearing/Feeling - Others hear the music, begin to free flow dance and develop the choreography by movement.

❺ For those who feel they have no repertoire of dance moves to draw from, please let me encourage you to begin to expose yourself to other means. Don't feel like all the movements have to be original or that you have to create them all, feel free to draw from others. I strongly suggest you obtain Christian dance videos (See resource

Three Types of Dancing

page), possibly enroll in a dance class at a local college or dance studio, or even seek out someone in your church who does have a background in dance.

❻ Also realize that there are major elements to be considered when choreographing. Some are:

☐ Symmetry: This is the balance or repetition of movement in a dance. Beware that too much of the same movement can be too monotonous and diminish the dances' effectiveness.

☐ Asymmetry: This is the unbalance or unexpected movement in a dance. Realize that the dance should have a continuity and if the movements are too diverse, then the unexpected can cause confusion.

☐ Dynamics: This is the energy in the dance. The energy of the dance is

Free To Dance

controlled by such things as posture, facial expressions, and choice of movements and how they are technically delivered.

☐ Levels: Levels are the different heights to which the dance is choreographed. It is good to put a variety of levels such as: high - up on toes with arms extended upwards; middle - kneeling; and low - bowing

☐ Range: Range is the size of the individual movement whether small or large. As an example, one could limit their hand movement only in front of their face versus extending the hands to the fullest extent of their arms.

☐ Direction: The direction is the angles to which the dance is choreographed. Such as movement as from front to back, left to right, or diagonally from corner to corner.

☐ Timing: This is the timing of a movement which can be crucial in mood setting and in giving greater meaning to the dance. As examples, some movements could be slow, slow and resisting, quick and strong, momentary pauses, etc.

SPONTANEOUS DANCE

G O D

PEOPLE

In spontaneous dance, the flow of communication and the expression of the heart is directed to God by both a single dancer, a dance team, or by an entire congregation.

Free To Dance

DEFINITION: A spontaneous dance is an unrehearsed dance arising from one's free will to express their hearts to God. This type of dance is not limited to just one individual but can be evidenced in a number of different arenas:

✱ It can be seen when an entire congregation spontaneously begins to praise the Lord in the dance.

✱ It can be seen when a dance team is given the liberty to exhort and encourage the congregation to enter in by spontaneously dancing before the people. [As an example, our dance team at Christian International, under the direction of the dance team leader, has the freedom to access the platform to spontaneously dance for the purpose of encouraging others to dance and to enhance the worship.]

✱ Or it can be unseen when one chooses to

Three Types of Dancing

express themselves during their private devotional worship before the Lord at home.

PRACTICAL INSIGHTS:

❶ It is important to know that we don't have to have the "Spirit come upon us" or have Holy Ghost "goose bumps" in order to initiate a spontaneous dance. Spontaneous dance can be an act of our will, motivated by a heart that desires to express love to God.

❷ Remember that worship is a function of the heart and the heart will find expression in a variety of external forms. Therefore we may flow in a variety of ways. **I encourage you to expand your vocabulary of movement, whereby giving more to draw from.** When I first began to dance, I purchased a book on sign language which is commonly incorporated in dance.

Free To Dance

❸ We must continue to realize that spontaneous dance doesn't give license or liberty for a dancer or dance team to override the anointing and flow of the service. As an example, if the flow of the worship service is quiet and reverent, one should not break forth into exuberant leaping and twirling. Also, having the liberty to spontaneously dance doesn't mean we do it whenever we desire, such as in the middle of a pastor's message. Of course, the majority of all spontaneous dance will be done during the praise and worship portion of a church service.

❹ If you feel like you would like to encourage someone to enter into spontaneous dance, please be sensitive to where they are at spiritually and mentally. It is important that we don't dominate others even if we feel we have developed a liberty to dance before the Lord.

❺ In order to experience a greater freedom

Three Types of Dancing

in spontaneous dance, it is important that the individual spends time in developing his/her personal relationship with the Lord. For it is out of this relationship of love that one overcomes all hindrances to freedom and has the ability to freely express themselves in the dance. "You shall know the truth [Jesus] and the truth will **make you free**." (John 8:32) A parallel of this principle can be found in human relationships. As a personal example, my children have great liberty in expressing their love to me. Not long ago, my oldest son, Aaron, said to me out of the blue with a big hug and kiss, "Your the best mommy in the world and my heart *beeps* for you!" Then my youngest son, Nathan grabbed both of my hands and kissed everyone of my fingers! Because of our relationship they know they have the freedom to express their love any time, any place and without any restrictions.

❻ Last, a spontaneous dancer must learn

the value of humility. The Bible states that God gives grace to the humble and it also encourages us to humble ourselves as a little child (Matthew 18:4). Many times children demonstrate to us a freedom to worship that far exceeds most adults due to their heart of humility and their absence of self-consciousness.

PROPHETIC DANCE

G O D

PEOPLE

In prophetic dance, the message originates with God and is communicated through the dancer(s) to the people..

Three Types of Dancing

DEFINITION: A prophetic dance is an unrehearsed/un-choreographed dance that is Holy Spirit directed which portrays a prophetic message to the people. Like prophecy, it is meant for the people at that particular place and time and serves to bring edification, exhortation and comfort. There is a difference between spontaneous dance and prophetic dance. Though both are spontaneous in nature, the prophetic dance communicates the heart of God and speaks His heart in "due season." (Job 42:5)

PRACTICAL INSIGHTS:

❶ We must realize that there are different ways to minister prophetic dance. Some of these are:

☐ A singer will begin to sing the Song of the Lord, (See suggested reading list for greater understanding of Song of the Lord) and a dancer will follow by interpreting the words being sung.

☐ It can also happen when a dancer begins to prophetically dance and then a singer will interpret the movements being portrayed in a prophetic song.

☐ It can happen when someone sings the song of the Lord and the dancer interprets the words **simultaneously** through movement, thus revealing to the dancer, singer and people that the ministry is being Holy Spirit orchestrated. I have even experienced, while ministering under this anointing, that my movements would actually come a few seconds before the singers words. Moving in this dimension does take a great "dance step" of faith but is truly awesome when it is experienced. (Rom. 12:6)

☐ It can happen when musicians are playing and prophesying with their instruments, and a dancer will interpret the notes with a prophetic dance. (1

Three Types of Dancing

Chronicles 25:1 and Psalm 149)

☐ It can happen when an individual prophesies, and a group or an individual dancer can act out by gesturing (Hosea 12:10 Amp.) through interpretive movement the prophetic word - even without music. Conversely, a group or individual dancer can act out a prophetic word and then someone can prophesy what was demonstrated.

☐ Last, a dancer or dance troupe may dance prophetically and the message is so clear to the people, that no interpretation by song or spoken word are necessary. In other words, the dance speaks for itself.

❷ Like prophecy, the prophetic dance should be ministered in due season. One should know the "house rules" of their local church to determine the timing of when to dance prophetically. In some churches it is proper protocol to check with either the dance team leader or whomever is the designated authority before going to the platform. Prophetic dance will enhance the attitude of worship rather than hinder it. In other words, just because one senses the unction to dance prophetically doesn't automatically mean that they should.

❸ Because prophetic dance is similar to prophecy, it takes time to grow in this realm. I would like to encourage the reader not to pressure themselves into feeling like they must be able to prophetically dance. Like prophecy, we minister in proportion to our faith and grace level. Romans 12:6 reveals that we prophesy according to our faith!

❹ The manifestation of prophetic dance is usually proceeded by someone who has taken the time to spiritually stir themselves. (2 Tim. 1:6) As one prays in the spirit or dances spontaneously, it can act as a catalyst to open one's heart for God to speak and minister in prophetic dance. It is important to exercise our discernment so that we can "tune in" to convey His heart in dance. (Hebrews 5:14)

Again, the three most common types of praise dance used in church ministry are:

1) CHOREOGRAPHED

2) SPONTANEOUS

3) PROPHETIC

Free To Dance

CHAPTER FOUR

OBSTACLES TO OVERCOME

"Who me, dance? You've got to be kidding! I'm not . . I can't . . I'm afraid . . " Do those words sound familiar? Whether one is on a dance team or is just beginning to dance before the Lord, there are always obstacles and hindrances to overcome. A classic example of overcoming obstacles can be found in the life of the great dancer Fred Astaire.

Free To Dance

After Fred Astaire's first screen test, the memo from the testing director of MGM, dated 1933, said, "Can't act! Slightly bald! Can dance a little!" Astaire kept that memo over the fireplace in his Beverly Hills home.

Like Fred Astaire, we must learn to overcome obstacles so that we can go on to be everything God has called us to be. Let's take a look at a few of the most common hurdles and how to overcome them.

OVERCOMING FEARS

Fear is the number one obstacle and hindrance to anyone desiring to dance. Fear has the ability to paralyze and immobilize and comes in many different forms. Let's investigate some of the ways that these fears could hinder your freedom in dance and the ways to overcome them:

Obstacles To Overcome

Fear of Looking Foolish: If most people were totally honest, they would agree that looking foolish in the dance is one of their greatest fears. Many are fearful that their movements won't look right or that they will appear to be awkward.

I recall not long ago, a pastor sharing an experience at a Promise Keeper's meeting. During the praise and worship he noticed a large man on the front row exuberantly worshiping the Lord in dance. The pastor related that as he watched the man dance in a seemingly awkward fashion (resembling an ostrich!), that he began to be embarrassed for the man's movements and seeming lack of control. Later, after the meeting while on the way home, the Lord began to convict the pastor for his attitude of judgment towards the man who danced so freely. The pastor said that eventually he was so convicted that he heard the Lord speak to him and say, "That man who you were judging in your heart tonight was very pleasing in My sight because

Free To Dance

he danced with his whole heart before Me." Then to his surprise, the Lord said to the pastor, "Would you dance like that for Me?" Later that evening, after arriving home, the pastor humbled himself and danced before the Lord for the first time! He testified later that while he danced before the Lord that night, a mighty and new presence of the Lord manifested in His life.

The questions is, will there be times when we might look awkward or lack grace? This is all subject to the opinion of man. But when it comes to worshiping God with all of our heart, it is the **opinion and approval of God** we need to seek after.

Some of you might feel that because of your appearance or your physique that you would look foolish dancing. But please keep your focus on the Lord and allow Him to minister to you through this scripture:

"Do not consider his

Obstacles To Overcome

appearance or his height for I have not rejected him. The Lord does not look at the things man looks at. Man looks at the outward appearance, but the Lord looks at the heart." 1 Sam. 16:7

Because dance is a free expression originating from the spirit of man and/or the Spirit of God, it can not be contained in what we feel or think is "the perfect look." While there are certain bodily movements which are un-Christlike and are suggestive in the wrong way, there are a wide range of movements which are not. [Every dancer should desire to improve their technique as long as the technique doesn't hinder their freedom in the Lord.]

Obviously David was not concerned in the least about looking foolish the day he danced before the ark in Jerusalem. He was so focused upon the Lord and the Lord's

Free To Dance

presence, He apparently didn't even care what the people thought. Even his own wife Michal found him to look foolish.

When it comes to looking "foolish," did you know t<s>hat it</s> *is* scriptural to look foolish? In Psalm 150:4 the Hebrew word for dance is halal which again means to shine, to boast, **to make a fool, to act madly!** So the next time the devil come to you and tells you that you look foolish, say to him, "It's in **the** Book and I'm a fool for Christ's sake for God has chosen the 'foolish' things to confound the wise!" (1 Cor. 1:25; 2:14; 4:10)

Fear of Making a Mistake: Like anything in life, mistakes will be made while dancing. I wish I could promise you a mistake-free experience but that is the ideal but it is not the real! At some time or another a dancer will forget part of the choreography, miss the timing, or maybe even trip. The important thing to remember is that it doesn't destroy the anointing and God is perfecting the Church

Obstacles To Overcome

through imperfect ministers and ministries.

The extreme fear of making a mistake can drive you to the "perfectionist syndrome." I experienced a time at the beginning of my dance training where I was driving myself into frustration by trying to clone myself after what I felt were "perfect dancers." I couldn't even watch myself on video without picking myself apart.

God took me to another extreme, which in the end broke the stronghold of perfectionism. I remember that while ministering at a church with my husband, I was asked to minister in dance before the ministry of the Word. I ministered a choreographed dance before the congregation that morning only to find out later that a portion of the back of my dress had gotten wedged and hung up in the top of my panty hose. Had I known it at the time, I would have cried! It wasn't until after the dance that I discovered what had happened.

Free To Dance

Through this incident, the Lord began to have me face my fear of making a mistake. It shattered my idealistic way of thinking that every thing had to be perfect in order to be anointed. I also realized that if I danced as unto the Lord with my whole heart and that it pleased Him, then why should I be hindered what others think or say. (I also learned to double check my dress before getting on the platform!)

Fear of the Unknown: Many times in ministry for the Lord, God will push you into realms where you have never been before. We must remember that he told Joshua that he was taking them in a "way they had never been before." Dancing is not an exception to this principle. Like the children of Israel, a dancer must be willing to walk by faith and not by sight.

As an example, when a dancer begins to minister in a prophetic dance, the first fear that he/she faces is the fear of not knowing if the movements will even come to mind. The opposite of fear is faith, so at times like this, we take the "leap of faith" into the unknown realm and allow the Holy Spirit to really take control.

Something that has helped me overcome this fear is **developing a love for the people that exceeds a love for myself**. Dancers must convince themselves that they are born to be a blessing and that their dance could be the blessing that someone needs to see. When we do this, we choose to move out in faith (motivated by a heart of love) to bless others. It is during these times that we discover that God responds and honors our acts of faith and obedience. He is soooo faithful!

Fear of Man: The fear of man can become a stronghold through a number of different factors. When a dancer begins to fear criticism, has a poor self-image, or feels like they are being rejected, it opens the door for a "man-pleasing" spirit to come in and build a

Free To Dance

stronghold in their mind. This spirit will snare the dancer into thinking they must have the approval of other people. (Remember, a man-pleasing spirit is what kept Moses out of the promised land! He was more concerned with the cry of the people than he was the destiny of God.) But Proverbs 29:25 says that "the fear of man brings a snare, but whoever puts his trust in the Lord will be safe."

Of course, no one wants to be rejected, judged, or made fun of but one must choose to please man or choose to please God. A dancer can not be concerned with peer pressure as it has held back countless saints from opening their hearts to the Lord.

Like Mary, when she let her hair down and wiped the master's feet, she experienced rejection and criticism by those who were with Jesus. She didn't follow the conventional form of worship and wasn't controlled by a man-pleasing spirit. Her love for the master and her corresponding actions drew great attention to

Obstacles To Overcome

herself that day (sometimes a dancer will draw great attention), yet she didn't allow the opinions of others to restrict her sincere act of worship. Regardless of her sinful past, she didn't allow it to taint her self-image. She expressed her love unashamedly before the Lover of her soul. (John 12 & Mark 14)

This area of "man-pleasing" is a place where I have had my greatest struggle. Dealing with this challenge has helped me discover some keys to overcoming. Here are some keys that I pray will help you if this is an area you struggle in also:

1) Face and admit your fear.
2) Remember **Who** you dance for!
3) Nurture your relationship with God so you will know His love for you - "Perfect love casts our fear." (1 John 4:18)
4) Know & trust the truth of the Scripture.
5) Receive encouragement from others.

Free To Dance

6) Renounce any covenant with fear.
7) Keep dancing regardless of how you feel!

Sometimes overcoming the fear of man is a long and challenging process. (It took the Lord forty years to get it out of the children of Israel in the desert!) But let me encourage you to say that as the "Joshua Generation", we can overcome this obstacle through God's grace.

OVERCOMING MIND-SETS

A second major hurdle to overcome when dancing is something we could term as "mind-sets." In other words, preconceived ideas that will or can eventually hinder us in our freedom to dance. Please allow me to list a few and how they are most likely to be expressed:

MIND-SET # 1

"I'm afraid I'll be a distraction or it might

bring too much attention to myself. It will cause people to focus more on me than on God!"

Most of the time this particular mind-set has its origin in the midst of the praise and worship portion of the service. As the congregation is worshiping, you might step to the platform to spontaneously dance/prophetically dance or by possibly leaving your row to dance in the aisle. You notice that others around you seem to be observing, more than entering into worship themselves. It is times like these when you may feel like a distraction.

The important thing to remember during these times is to keep your focus on the Lord and remember that the worship service is designed for worshipers! It is the designated time to praise God in **all** the scriptural forms of worship.

A second thing to remember is that if you

Free To Dance

allow this mind-set to hinder you, it will bring bondage to you by not allowing you to express your passion to the Lord. How others view you is not the important aspect - it's how God sees you!

Please note that I am not suggesting anyone "take over the platform and run the show." Freedom to dance in a congregational meeting is always based upon submission to leadership and the flow of the Holy Spirit. Again, every worshiper should know the "rules of the house" so that leadership guidelines will direct and channel your freedom, not quench it.

**A NOTE TO THOSE THAT ARE DISTRACTED BY THOSE WHO DANCE - IF YOU FIND YOURSELF BEING DISTRACTED BY OTHERS, YOU MIGHT CHOOSE TO CHANGE YOUR PERSPECTIVE BY ALLOWING THE DANCER/S TO BECOME AN INSPIRATION FOR YOUR PERSONAL WORSHIP OR YOU MIGHT CHOOSE TO KEEP YOUR EYES CLOSED ALTOGETHER. I'D LIKE TO REMIND YOU THAT DAVID'S TABERNACLE WAS A PLACE OF

Obstacles To Overcome

VIBRANT, LOUD AND **DEMONSTRATIVE** WORSHIP.

MIND-SET # 2

"I'm having personal struggles in my life and don't feel worthy enough to dance."

Because dance is a more "visible" form of worship in the church, the dancer's attitudes and actions may be scrutinized more than the other more conservative worshipers. Some might look at a dancer and say, "I know that brother/sister 'so and so' is having integrity problems . . . or marriage problems, etc."

Every worshiper must realize that we do not worship the Lord based upon our own righteousness or good works. Who is not working through at least one area of weakness in their life? At what point in our spiritual growth are we "mature enough" or "holy enough" to worship the Lord in the dance? Is dance a greater expression of worship than

Free To Dance

clapping or kneeling? Of course not! Worshiping the Lord in the dance isn't based upon our spiritual maturity or our own righteousness. It is based upon the fact that we are righteous through Him and He is worthy to be praised. (Is 64:6)

There is a time when one might step down from a "visible" position in a dance team. It is when a member of a dance team has an area in their life that is in need of restoration and deliverance. This decision must rest upon the shoulders of church leadership. Every dancer should realize that a great mark of maturity will be their ability to "lay down their ministry" for a season until the Lord has time to heal and/or deliver.

MIND-SET # 3

"I have done a lot of worldly dancing in my past and I am concerned my movements will reflect the spirit of the world."

Obstacles To Overcome

Sometimes when one has danced in the "world" it becomes hard to dance before the Lord. Be careful not to link your current identity (that is now "in Christ") with your unrenewed past life. It is like those who have played musical instruments in worldly bands and night clubs but who have dedicated their talent to the Lord and are now blessings in the local church. We must remember that II Cor. 5:17 states that *"If any man be in Christ, he is a new creature: old things are passed away; behold are things are become new."*

It reminds me of the story of the man that captured the wild eagle and tethered the great bird to a small radius. Everyday the bird tried to fly off but his movements were continually restricted by his environment. Years later, the bird was sold to a new owner who immediately untethered the bird and expected it to fly off. To his amazement, the bird just flew in the same radius as it had when it was tethered. It had been so conditioned by its past that it didn't recognize the freedom that

<u>Free To Dance</u>

was returned to it.

Like the great eagle, a dancer can be tethered to their past and their movements can be restricted if they haven't taken the time to renew their minds with the Word (Romans 12:2).

Of course, they are some dance gestures and movements which are sensual and not conducive to Godly worship. I would suggest that those who are not sure about certain movements should 1) review their movements in front of a mirror or 2) be open to input from church leadership.

MIND-SET # 4

"I have no dance training and I feel inadequate."

The important thing to remember here is that God is not looking for trained dancers who must learn how to worship. Instead He is

Obstacles To Overcome

seeking worshipers who desire to learn how to dance.

Sometimes trained dancers require an extra measure of grace because they can become too self-confident. God wants us to come to a place that our confidence is found in Him.

We must remember that everyone is at a different stage of development and God has not given everyone the same measure of skill. The Bible states, *"For who has despised the day of small things."* (Zech. 4:10) As the old Chinese proverbs states, "All start at the bottom and work up." Keep in mind that discouragement in dance many times comes to us because we compare our skill level with others. Wherever you may be in your stage of dance development, I encourage you to press onward.

I want to encourage you to keep your eyes focused on Him as you grow in your natural dance abilities. Remember that not all dancers

Free To Dance

are called to be "professionals" and one must be content with the level of grace and skill God has granted. Some are graced with the great natural ability to dance but whatever level of skill you have been given, remember - do your best with what ability you presently have.

I do believe that God is requiring a spirit of excellence from all His ministries but we must realize that Biblical excellence is not based upon performance, but upon a willingness to try to do our best.

MIND-SET # 5

"I'm too old to dance!"

This is a common misconception that I hear when traveling to do dance workshops since I work with a variety of age groups. When people express this mind-set to me, I quickly remind them that dance knows no age limit. Even in the secular environment, people of all ages dance at weddings and enjoy styles such as ballroom dancing and /or line-dancing.

Jeremiah 31:13 states: *"Then shall the maidens rejoice in the dance, and the **young** men and **old** together..."*

Of course, those who are older in age might not want to jump right in to a fast paced jazz class. They may prefer even the style of Jewish folk dancing or slower interpretive dance.

Whatever your age, don't feel that dance is not for you. It is a matter of finding which style and pace you feel most physically capable of.

MIND-SET # 6

"The Jewish style folk-dance or slow interpretive dance is the more anointed form of dance."

While I am sure the Lord takes pleasure in

Free To Dance

seeing the above two forms of dance, we must remember that He is the Lord of the dance . . . . in **all** its forms. To say that one style of dance is more anointed or more powerful is in reality one's personal preference rather than the measure of anointing and power.

Since one of the primary purposes of dance is to communicate, we must realize that different styles of dance have the ability to communicate different moods, tones, and messages.

As an example, a very upbeat, high energy dance may convey the joy of the Lord or possibly spiritual warfare. While a slower style normally carries with it such themes as mercy, intimacy, love, forgiveness, compassion, etc.

Therefore, I would strongly urge every dancer to keep an open heart and mind towards the various styles of dance, realizing that God is creative and diverse in all that He does.

Obstacles To Overcome

IN SUMMARY: I haven't listed all the obstacles to dance, but I chose to list some of the most common hurdles. If any of these obstacles stand out to you, I would encourage you to allow time, grace, study of the Word, and prayer to give you grace and courage to overcome any hindrances. Most importantly know that "what is impossible with men is possible with God." (Luke 18:27)

In the next chapter, let's venture into the realm of the heart of the praise dancer.

Free To Dance

CHAPTER FIVE

PERFORMANCE VS MINISTRY

[THE HEART OF THE DANCER]

One of the greatest struggles for the dancer and one of the areas of concern for church leadership is whether the dancer will be able to dance out of a pure motive and a right spirit.

I, like you, have seen some who have been involved in worship who started out with the

Free To Dance

right spirit but unfortunately began to lose their ministry perspective and begin to enter into pride. There is no doubt that the area of worship (arts) is very susceptible to the lure of fame and ego. One only has to remember Lucifer's ministry in Heaven to remember how pride caused the fall and failure of his eternal ministry before God.

In this chapter I would like to discuss that I believe dance starts in the heart, not in the feet! Psalm 9:1 states, *"I will praise you Oh Lord with all my heart."*

The most vital part of the dance ministry lies within the heart of the dancer. To me, the heart of the dancer is formed by three major areas: **will, emotions** and **beliefs**.

It is the responsibility of every potential worshiper (dancer) to guard their heart. We are commanded by God in Proverbs 4:23, *"Keep thy **heart** with all diligence; for out of it are the issues of life."*

Performance Vs Ministry

A worshiper must minister out of a true heart for God. If not, then one is in danger of going through the motions without heart worship.

In Matthew Chapter 15:7 & 8, Jesus very clearly reveals why those in Isaiah's day were hypocrites or play actors. He states: *"Ye hypocrites, well did Esaias prophesy of you saying, This people draweth nigh unto me with their mouth, and honoureth me their lips; but their heart is far from me."*

The desire of every dancer should be to minister from a pure heart that is not tainted by pride, ego, jealousy, selfish ambition, self-promotion, etc. As Andrew Murray once so clearly stated about the heart:

> "In man's nature the heart is the central power. As the heart is so is the man . . . our inmost being must in truth be yielded to Him . . . It is only as the desire of the heart is fixed upon God, the whole heart seeking for God, giving

its love and finding its joy in God, that a man can draw nigh to God."

Therefore, as you can see, keeping our mind focused and our heart pure before the Lord is the responsibility of every dancer.

Let's go on to discuss some areas which I believe can help us all keep a pure motive and right spirit before the Lord in our ministry.

KNOWING GOD & HIS WORD

There is a big difference between knowing about God and <u>knowing</u> Him. Remember, many lost people say that they know God but in reality they do not. Knowing God is based upon intimacy and a real relationship, so it is important that we press into Him and <u>seek</u> after the Lord. As we do, then we will have the ability to impart His nature and character to those whom we minister.

Performance Vs Ministry

In John 4:23 & 24 it states,

> *"Yet a time is coming and has now come when the true worshipers will worship the Father in **spirit** and in **truth**, for they are the kind of worshipers the Father seeks. God is spirit and his worshipers must worship in **spirit** and in **truth**.."* (NIV)

In this scripture, I believe we could relate the word *spirit* to the human spirit which deals with our motive and right attitude. Our dance, as a form of worship, must come from an outflow of genuine expression from a heart that knows God. Not only should we dance with the right *spirit*, but of course, we should minister based upon our knowledge of the *truth* of who He is.

SELF-EVALUATION

I believe another key to keeping a right motive and heart in worship is to peek into the

Free To Dance

windows of our heart and allow the Lord to minister to us on such issues as priorities, seasons, obstacles, etc.

These are times when we ask ourselves the hard questions such as:

"When I dance, am I feeding more on the attention I may get from the people, than on God?"

"Do I have to be complemented on every thing I do?"

"Do I get jealous when someone gets a promotion on the dance team?"

"Am I intimidated or envious over the skills of another dancer?"

"Do I have to be 'perfect' in everything I do?"

"Am I so anxious for God to use me in the dance that I find myself striving beyond God's

timing, will, and grace."

"Am I spending enough time with the Lord in prayer and in His Word?"

"Are there any unresolved issues in my life that are causing bitterness or unforgiveness?"

"Is my schedule too busy?"

"Have I been dancing before the Lord in my private devotional time?"

"Have I been obedient in the areas in which God has been speaking to me?"

"Do I have a teachable spirit that is able to receive?"

YIELDING TO GOD'S DEALINGS

As God speak to us we must, as clay, be willing to yield to the pressure of the potter's hand. The Lord will allow the pressures of life, the testings of God , and even "sandpaper" people that can help smooth out our character to surface certain heart issues and attitudes.

We must remember that Jeremiah 17:9 states that the heart of man is deceitful above all things. God allows pressure in our lives so that hidden weaknesses and poor attitudes can be forced to the surface so that we might face them and deal with them.

Therefore, it is important to exercise our spiritual ears so that we can tune in and understand the dealings of God in our life. When we understand and respond correctly to the pressures and test of life, it will release a heart that can rejoice in all things, (even in the midst of trials and tribulations) and will develop in us the character to maintain a ministry based upon servanthood, not performance. Confusion, doubt and fear can enter into ones' heart if the seasons of life and testings of God are not clearly understood.

STIRRING A PASSION FOR GOD

Last, in order to develop and maintain a ministry based upon servanthood, I believe it is critical that every dancer should cultivate a passion for God - a heart that is fully devoted to and has an ardent affection for God.

Here are a few things which I believe will help cultivate one's passion for the Lord:

#1 A PRAYERFUL HEART - We have heard the exhortation to pray so much that we have almost become immune to its importance. But we must not let it escape our priority list.

#2 A TRUSTING HEART - Our passion for the Lord will be kindled when we really begin to believe that "He that has begun a good work in us, will see it through to the day of Jesus Christ." (Phil. 1:6)

#3 AN UNDISTRACTED HEART - We can not allow the cares of this life and life's

Free To Dance

distractions to hinder our focus on Him. As an example, as a creative type personality, I can sometimes read an entire page of a book but not know one thing that I have read. While reading, my mind will begin to wander and become distracted by such thoughts as , "What am I going to get at the grocery store." This can also happen to us while we worship the Lord. We may dance outwardly but inwardly our hearts and minds might be "dancing to a different tune."

#4 AN UNDIVIDED HEART - An undivided heart is one which is committed. In order to see passion continue to grow, it is important that our heart stay singular focused on the things of God. We must stay committed to fellowship, the word, prayer, and scheduled church activities such as dance practice/worship practice.

#5 A MOTIVATED HEART - It is important by an act of your own will to keep yourself stirred. I have found that in my life there are a number of things that motivate me and keep me stirred up for God. Some of these are contemporary Christian music, listening to a motivational Christian speaker, reading a book that is applicable to where I am at, or attending a Christian conference.

#6 A VISIONARY HEART - Some times, our passion is based upon an ability to see what God is doing in and around us. We should hunger and seek to see our own potential and the potential of those around us. We should also look to continue to see God's desire, design and development for His church.

In conclusion, what makes a performer different from a minister? Please allow me to sum it up with these following comparisons:

A performer's motive is to awe and impress his audience - a ministers motive and desire is to bless and edify his audience.

Free To Dance

A performer's reward is the applause of man - a ministers reward is the approval of God.

A performer will dance for his own gratification - a minister will dance with God's purpose & vision.

A performer is anxious over the outcome of his dance - a minister prays and leaves the results to God.

A performer is consumed with perfection - a minister's desire is to see the audience turn their eyes in Christ's direction.

CHAPTER SIX

DYNAMICS OF DANCE TEAM MINISTRY

In this chapter I would like to reveal a number of different aspects in regards to formulating and developing a dance team in the local church. There is no doubt that "team ministry" is scriptural and is God's design for today's 21st Church.

I am sure some leaders are asking, "What is the purpose of dance team ministry? Why should we make an effort to develop a dance team? I know there might be a few benefits, but aren't there great risks?"

Let's commence this chapter with a brief look at the **purpose** for formulating a dance team. Formulating a dance team will serve some of the following purpose:

PURPOSES

#1 - Formulating a dance team will provide a balanced, safe, and structured environment for training those who have a great desire to dance.

#2 - Formulating a dance team will enhance the existing worship in the local church. Dance can stir the Church to respond to the fullness of God's manifest presence.

3 - Formulating a dance team can provide an outlet for those gifted and called into arts.

#4 - Formulating a dance team can also

Dynamics of Team Ministry

provide an opportunity for youth to get involved in expressive worship. Many leaders are looking for ways and means to get their young people involved and committed to God. Providing them with an opportunity to join a dance team can help focus their energies towards something that has eternal value.

Now, lets look at some risks involved in formulating a dance team in the local church:

RISKS

#1 - There is the risk that a dance team will only become an "entertainment team", rather than a part of the worship team.

#2 - There is the risk that the team will become a "clique" and will exclude the value of congregational dancing.

#3 - There is the risk that the "team" might become so talented that they have a vision

Free To Dance

to separate and start their "own ministry."

#4 - There is the risk that the dancers could become "super-spiritual" in their ministry. As an example I've heard of one team that actually left the church service, changed into their dance outfits and paraded back into the service to "interpret" the pastor's message while he was still preaching!

#5 . . . . etc, etc, etc

As you can see, the list could continue on, but I believe the rewards of formulating a dance team far outweigh the risks. Keep in mind that risks can be minimized when a **proper foundation** and **proper training** is imparted to the people and to the beginning dance team members. [Hence, this is one of the purposes for writing this book.]

I strongly recommend that the leadership of the local church invite someone in who has dance team experience to help formulate and discuss these types of issues.

FORMULATING A TEAM

Now let's look at formulating a team in the local church. Later we will discuss the role of the leader and the role of the dancers and other critical issue. Please note that the following format is not to be a slave pattern but a *suggested* format.

The genesis of any dance team first starts with vision. The leadership of the local church must share with the people the vision to develop dance and dance team ministry. As the vision is shared, the Holy Spirit will begin to speak to the hearts of those who have a desire to grow in dance ministry.

Next, leadership must discern and choose someone whom they feel has the ability, maturity, and the heart to lead the team. This person doesn't necessarily have to have an extensive background in dance but must have

Free To Dance

enough gifting and grace to ignite and train others. [Please note that I will discuss in greater detail the role of the leader later on.]

After the leader is chosen, I would suggest that:

> 1) a designated night be set aside for those to attend who feel called in this area. Prior to the meeting, a sign-up sheet could be posted in the church foyer which should include such information as name, phone number, and prior dance experience. At this meeting, the designated team leader will again impart the vision, then go over team requirements, and then pass out a dance team practice schedule. Also it might be good to have each individual write out their own personal expectations, vision, and desires for being a part of a dance team.
>
> 2) all guidelines, requirements, policies

and vision be put in writing. Every potential member of the team should have their own copy to help alleviate any future mis-communication.

The next phase of development will be to decide if your team is large enough to separate into skill levels or age groups. My recommendation is that each leader be flexible in their approach to assigning people to dance categories. For example, I have seen 12 to 14 year old dancers whose skill levels were equal to those in their late twenties and whose maturity was developed enough to handle this level of team ministry.

If however, your initial team is small in number but has a diversity of abilities, don't be discouraged. There are ways to choreograph dance pieces which can include all levels of skill, age and size.

After your first initial meeting, the team leader then discusses the practical issues such as

Free To Dance

what to wear, when to practice, how long to practice, and how often to practice. My suggestion is that you meet at least one time each week for a few hours. Of course, special events such as conferences, Christmas and Easter specials may require more practice time.

Finally, I would like to share some practical insights in regards to dance team ministry. These are based upon some of the most commonly asked questions I receive while doing local church dance seminars.

PRACTICAL INSIGHTS

"What kind of requirements should I place on my team?"

There are a number of different areas that are essential for seeing the vision of a team fulfilled. Some of these are:

ATTENDANCE - It is important that

team members are committed to attend scheduled practices. Yet at the same time, grace should be extended to those who have a viable excuse not to attend. I recommend that each member be given the phone number of the team leader and that if a member is unable to attend practice, they would call in advance. Of course, if someone constantly misses practices, then the team leader should remind the individual of the written guidelines.

DRESS - Again, a clear written policy on dress standards should be communicated. There are certain basic undergarments that should be worn by women that promote modesty. Some of these would be double lined sports bras, tights, and if wearing shorts - bikers shorts underneath. In regards to outer garments, make sure your neck line is not too low and revealing and that your garments are not too tight. Dress comfortable but modest. Remember, you're not there to display your body but for your body to display biblical truths and bring glory to God! I strongly suggest that all costumes and dress ideas should be shared with the senior pastor to make sure it meets with his/her approval. Remember, the leadership of the church will receive the criticism for allowing something to take place in church that the congregation feels is not modest or appropriate for presentation in a public church service.

BIBLE FOUNDATION - Each team member should be ready to explain the biblical basis for the arts in ministry.

"What will create an atmosphere of unity in my team?"

No doubt, there are things which will "tie" a team together or "tear" a team apart.

Dynamics of Team Ministry

☺ HERE ARE THINGS THAT **TIE**:

PRAYING FOR ONE ANOTHER - On regular basis set aside 10 minutes so that team members can pair off and pray for one another.

GROUP DISCUSSIONS - Occasionally have group discussion times with such topics as: Facing Your Fears; Discouragement; Personal Testimonies; etc.

TEAM LEADER SHARING: On a weekly basis the team leader should share 10-15 minutes from their heart.

PLAY TIME - Every team should schedule periodic times when they gather outside the local church to engage in fun activities.

CONTRIBUTION TIME - A team will

definitely feel more unified when each member is allowed to "buy into the vision." "Buying in" is when each member is allowed to have verbal input into such areas as choreography, costume ideas, spiritual insights, music selection, etc.

TIMES OF ENCOURAGING ONE ANOTHER - Because different members are at different skill levels, everyone should be exhorted to encourage one another. As an example, you might have feelings of jealousy towards another member of the dance team that seems to have greater skills. Rather than brood and cultivate envy towards them, I would encourage you to approach this particular person and even ask for their help. Facing your feelings head-on and addressing the other person will greatly aid in overcoming jealousy.

☹ HERE ARE THINGS THAT **TEAR**:

CARNAL COMPETITION - As we will address in greater detail in the next chapter, a spirit of competition always begin when we compare ourselves among ourselves. Competition always leads to jealousy, envy, gossip and strife. However, being motivated to do better by watching another excel in excellence is good.

CLIQUES - Every member should be encouraged not to exclude others. It is vitally important to make other team members feel like they belong!

PRIDE - Nothing can tear a team apart faster than when certain members become prideful of their talents and abilities. It can be evidenced when someone says, "I should always be in the front." Or they might say, "I'm the best dancer on the team and I have more dance experience than anyone else!" If you feel like you must always be seen, then I would strongly suggest that you do an inward evaluation of your motive for dancing.

"How do you get team members to take it seriously? Some just see it as fun and games."

I suggest that on an on-going basis the team leader speak the purpose and vision of the team. The team members need to hear on a regular basis the validity and value of dance and the fact that their ministry is as "unto the Lord." I would also recommend that the dance team leader invite the church leadership to speak to the dance team members a number of times each year so that the team members hear the heart of the church leadership team. At that time, the church leadership can continue to encourage the team. They can also validate how *serious* and *important* the dance team ministry is and how important it is for each member to keep the right heart and attitude.

BEING AN EFFECTIVE DANCE TEAM LEADER

In this section I would like to share some attributes which I feel are characteristic of an effective dance team leader. While I feel that all these qualities are important, we also must not loose sight of the fact that every leader is also in the process of personal development and in leadership development Understanding this will keep us from becoming critical of those whom the Lord has chosen to bring oversight into our lives.

SERVANTHOOD - A great mark of spiritual maturity will be the leaders ability to serve the team. (Mat. 20:27) Leaders are commanded to lead by example, not by lording.(1 Peter 5:3)

Free To Dance

Nothing will stifle the creativity of a team more than a leader who rules with an iron fist and a harsh spirit. Remember, the team leader will in many ways act as an "under-shepherd" under the senior pastor. For that reason, they must be willing to sacrificially give of their time and energy to each team member. They must develop the attitude that the team is working with them, not for them.

SHARING HONOR - An effective team leader should share his honor with the rest of the team. The team leader should verbally honor them, stating how much he/she appreciates them and recognizing them for a job well done.

RECOGNIZING DANCER'S POTENTIAL - The leader should never loose sight of the fact that they are there to help others reach their full potential. As Dr. Costa Deir once stated, "A wise leader who concentrates on correcting and helping the marginal performer, rather than giving up on him, may turn him into an excellent producer with surprising results: never give up on people until you have done your best for them." A wise leader will recognize the unique strengths of each individual team member. As an example, one may be more gifted in jazz, while another more gifted in ballet. Or perhaps, the leader might discover that someone less skilled in dance ability might actually have a great creative ability to choreograph or design costumes. I have known many choreographers who were not the best dancers.

REPRODUCING THEMSELVES - An effective leader will have a vision of multiplying their ministry. They will be willing to delegate responsibility and authority to others while also maintaining accountability. They have a heart to take risk and to trust team members so that the team members can rise to new levels.

ADMITTING MISTAKES - Since leaders are all "subject to like passions" (Jas. 5:17), every

Free To Dance

leader will make a mistake such as losing their temper, cutting someone off, or making a poor judgment. A wise leader will be transparent before the team and humble enough to admit a mistake.

COMMUNICATES - An effective leader always leaves lines of communication open with the team. They will create an atmosphere in which each team member will feel comfortable enough and safe enough to approach and share their views without fear of retribution. A reasonable leader will create a safe environment that allows others to vent their feelings, whether positive or negative, thus giving them the same privileges he/she would give themselves. Last, a good communicator will be able to convey their thoughts in a tactful manner, while validating the views of others and stressing the points he agrees on. In doing so, it will continue to engender open communication with the team.

ENCOURAGES CREATIVITY - A

discerning leader will give much room for flexibility so that each team member will be creative. Creativity should be directly encouraged within the boundaries of good judgment. Again, Dr. Deir once stated, "A wise leader refrains from treating people like puppets, but rather he gives them opportunity to think and have a part in planning the details of the responsibilities so they can develop their latent abilities." We must never forget that dance is an art, as well as a ministry, and thrives upon a creative atmosphere.

DOESN'T SHOW FAVORITES - Showing favorites is a death toll to team unity. A wise leader will not be a respecter of people, regardless of their stature or their abilities. They will be able to make each dancer feel worthy and special in their individual place of contribution thereby fulfilling Eph. 4:16 - *"From whom the whole body fitly joined together and compacted by that which every joint supplieth, according to the effectual working of the measure of every part, maketh increase of the body unto the edifying of itself in love."*

SENSITIVITY - A sensitive leader is insightful enough to pinch himself once in a while so that he knows how others feel. They will seek to understand people and be willing to look through the eyes of others.

BRINGS CORRECTION - A loving leader will also be a leader capable of confronting and correcting with a loving but firm demeanor. As was once stated, "Blessed is the leader who raises his voice to soprano in praise and lowers it to bass when he needs to correct the situation, for he shall have greater results."

FOLLOW THE LEADER

In order to be an effective team, it not only takes a good leader, but also good followers. Let's go over some of the characteristics of effective team members.

Dynamics of Team Ministry

COMMITTED - Every member of the dance team should be committed to the team, to the vision of the dance troupe, and to the leadership of the church. Commitment will be the glue that holds the team together during times of stress, strain, and seasons of intensity.

TEACHABLE SPIRIT - A key to becoming a great team player is allowing God to work within you the attribute of having a teachable, adjustable, submissive, and flexible attitude. A great hindrance to growing in dance ministry is when someone develops an unwillingness to receive input in important areas such as dance technique and/or character issues. Every member must be open to the critiquing of their style or attitude without feeling like they are being rejected or criticized. A submissive attitude will exhibit itself by saying things such as, "If you see anything in my life that could hinder me or hurt others, please love me enough to share it with me." Also, displaying a flexible attitude will be necessary because every dance team

Free To Dance

will face situations which are not always the most ideal. As an example, I have had to practice and dance on cramped platforms, in hot buildings, and on poor flooring. A teachable and flexible spirit will be content in all situations, while those who are un-flexible will always whine and complain.

ENERGY AND ENTHUSIASM - Team members need to display an attitude of self-motivation coupled with energy and an enthusiastic demeanor.

ATTENTIVE - It is important to display a respectful attitude towards your team leader and fellow dance team members. For example, while the leader is talking and instructing, all focus should be upon the team leader.

SUPPORTIVE ATTITUDE - Team members should be willing to contribute to other necessary duties such as clean-up, special phone call assignments, car pooling, etc.

Dynamics of Team Ministry

HUMBLE - A humble attitude is an admirable and important attribute that is demonstrated in such areas as:
- ▸ Willing to serve in any area
- ▸ Willing to allow others to go first
- ▸ Willing to be transparent before leadership

ACCOUNTABLE - The team members must see their place of ministry as a place of personal accountability to God and also to the team. Accountability is based upon humility and teachability but will be evidenced in areas such as open communication with leadership and fellow team members. Things such as personal struggles, offenses, and any type of conflict should be brought to leadership for the sake and safety of counsel.

PATIENCE - We must all be willing to wait upon the timing of the Lord for promotion. Our gifts and talents will make room for us but the Lord loves us enough not to push us out beyond our level of grace and maturity.

IN CLOSING

Being a part of dance team ministry has many benefits. It is a place to:

- experience a sense of joy and fulfillment.
- be challenged, groomed, and seasoned.
- develop relational skills.
- receive encouragement.
- exercise and stay in good physical shape.
- learn and increase in dance skills.
- find your potential and your place.
- to be mentored and discipled.

Let's go on to the final chapter and discover what it means to have excellence in your dance ministry.

CHAPTER SEVEN

DANCING WITH EXCELLENCE

In closing, I would like to encourage and challenge all those who desire to dance to do it with excellence. Whether you are worshiping the Lord in the congregation or on an established dance team, I believe the Lord desires that all that we do, we do with a spirit of excellence.

In order to achieve biblical excellence, we must understand what it is. In doing so, it will guard us against pride, ego and the sin of comparing ourselves against others.

DEFINING EXCELLENCE

I believe that Christian excellence is not a vicious competitiveness with others but a personal commitment to becoming the best one can be - **under the banner of God's grace**. It is not just the achievement of great skills, but it is the ongoing pursuit of everything within us to achieve Christ's character and ministry. Col. 3:23 states, "Whatever you do, work at it with **all your heart**, as working for the Lord, not for men." (NIV)

The world defines excellence in a number of different ways. Some describe excellence as talents or achievements, but even if those achievements help mankind, they are of no merit unless they have eternal value.

Others define excellence based upon one's

Dancing With Excellence

purpose. As an example, if a knife cuts well, then it is said to be excellent. Philosopher's of old stated that man's excellence was found in his capacity for rational thought. In other words, human achievement through intelligence and reasoning was said to make one excellent. The only problem is that it leaves out the work of the Holy Spirit and God's grace.

For others, the pursuit of excellence is based upon "success in life." Those that expound these ideas are in love with "self-realization" and "self-actualization." While I whole heartedly agree with running to discover one's potential, I don't agree with discovering our potential to the degree that we leave God's divine work of faith and grace in the dust.

One of the last approaches to excellence is that we have excellence when we concentrate on skills. These skills can be exhibited in such areas as athletics, science and, yes, the arts! Unfortunately, in most cases, character is not a primary factor. Men and women are praised for excellence in business when they can produce money. The athlete is praised for his excellence when he can catch the football at the sound of the buzzer and make the winning touchdown. The educator is praised when he can motivate his students at all costs to achieving "good grades." And yes, the dancer is praised for excellence when their performance is flawless.

While excellence of achievement and performance is desirable, we can lose sight of the "big picture" if we are not careful. We must remember that skill without character can give overnight fame, but it doesn't build the longevity of greatness. Greatness in God only comes from allowing the Holy Spirit to continually work in our lives and in our ministry. Remember, there have been many "superstars" in every arena of life who have displayed great talent, great ability, great skill and have become household names overnight, but over a process of time their private lives were revealed as less than admirable.

One must remember that excellence of character takes priority over excellence of achievement. Your position in dance is not just to dance, but it is to become a Godly worshiper who expresses themselves to God and to His people through the medium of dance *with* the character of Jesus.

EXCELLENCE DEMANDS RESPONSIBILITY

We are to take whatever talents and abilities God has gifted us with and invest them into the Kingdom of God. Like the parable of talents (Mat. 25), each dancer has stewardship responsibilities over the graces that have been given. As we accept the responsibility to give ourselves wholeheartedly to God's purpose and exercise our gifts and abilities within the range of our responsibilities, we then will have achieved excellence.

Free To Dance

Keep in mind that the title of "excellence" isn't just for those who have the most talent (5 talents man), but is based upon taking what we have been graced with and utilizing it. Remember, the two-talent man in this parable received the same reward as the five-talent man! Your abilities might be less than another dancer, but if we are responsible to use whatever talent we have been given to the best of our abilities and maturity, then we are operating in the realm of true excellence.

Yes, God's concept of excellence is quite different from the world's point of view. The dancer must renew his/her mind that:

There is a different standard of excellence in the Kingdom - <u>God</u>.

There is a different goal of excellence in the Kingdom - <u>Christlikeness</u>.

There is a different focus for excellence - <u>character</u>.

Dancing With Excellence

There is a different motive for excellence - God's glory.

There is a different enablement for excellence - God's grace.

There is a different model of excellence - Christ.

There is a different foundation for excellence - the Word of God.

Recently the Olympics were held in our neighboring state, Georgia. As most people know, the slogan for the athletes is always "Go for the Gold!" My prayer is that this book will inspire you to continue to go for the gold of excellence in your life and ministry. And last, if dance is in your heart, then break the chains of fear and inhibition, allow excellence to arise, and be released to be *free to dance!*

SUGGESTED READING LIST

1) <u>Restoring Praise & Worship to the Church</u>, Edited by David K. Blomgren, Dean Smith & Douglas Christoffel, 1989, Revival Press - Destiny Image Publishers, P.O. Box 351, Shippenburg, PA 17257 ISBN #0-938612-40-9

2) <u>How To Worship Jesus Christ</u>, By Joseph S. Carroll, 1984, Riverside Press, Memphis, TN

3) <u>Silencing the Enemy</u> by Robert Gay, Prophetic Praise Ministries, 1995, Creation House, Orlando, FL ISBN# 0-88419-349-7

4) <u>The Eternal Church</u> by Dr. Bill Hamon, 1981, Christian International Ministries, P.O. Box 9000, Santa Rosa Beach, FL 32459 ISBN# 0-939868-00-8

5) <u>Creative Journey</u> by Sharon Potter, 1996, Breakthrough Ministries, 2932 Nicely Ct., Dumfries, VA 22026

6) <u>The Tabernacle of David</u> by Kevin J. Conner, 1976, Bible Temple Publications, Portland, Oregon 97213, ISBN#0-914926-19-0

7) <u>Exploring Worship</u> by Bob Sorge, 1987, Son-Rise Publications, Rte.3, Box 202, New Wilmington, PA 16142, ISBN #0-936369-04-3

8) <u>Called, Appointed, Anointed</u> by Janny Grein, 1981, Foundation Ministries, Box 70, Bixby, OK 74008

9) <u>The Dynamics of Team Ministry</u> by David Blomgren, 1994, Treasure House, P.O. Box 310, Shippensburg, PA 17257, ISBN#1-56043-807-X

EXPAND YOUR DANCE WORKSHOPS

Eileen's dance workshops can be tailored to meet your individual needs but they are all designed to:

- To inspire and impart a new freedom, so that each participant can express themselves to the glory of God through dance.
- To expand the participants creativity of movements through technical training.
- To experience spontaneous dance activations.
- To teach a new choreographed dance which the students can perform.

Eileen's workshops can be performed in a 3 to 8 hour format, depending upon the depth, skill, and desire of the participants.

For more information, please call (850)267-2641, E Mail: DSchu99282@aol.com or write Preparing The Way Ministries, P.O. Box 1711, Santa Rosa Beach, FL 32459

Biographical Sketch of the Schultz's

Steve and Eileen Schultz are apostolic/prophetic servants of the Lord with a background marked with diverse service in the Body of Christ. Steve has been actively serving the Lord in full-time ministry since 1982. Since his start in ministry, he has faithfully served in various ministry positions such as an associate pastor, administrator, director of ministry of helps, crusade coordinator and as a missions director for World Outreach Ministries, Marietta, Georgia. Each step of progression has helped broaden and diversify his anointing, gifting and calling as a prophet. Eileen has co-labored as a mother, homemaker, as a minister in dance and in singing and is raising two sons, Aaron and Nathan. Eileen has a special anointing to instruct dance and offers "Expand Your Dance" workshops for local church dance teams.

Steve and Eileen currently serve as full-time traveling ministers and members of Christian International's Ministries Board of Govenors. Their ministry thrust is best summarized in 2 Peter 1:12; that the Body of Christ today "...*be established in present truth.*" They are assisting pastors around the world in developing strong united churches which function and operate in present truth. Eileen's greatest desire is to see people set free in the arts so that they can fully express themselves towards God and fully express God's heart to His people.

For More Information On Hosting an "EXPAND YOUR DANCE WORKSHOP" in your local church, please contact Eileen Schultz at: Preparing the Way Ministries, P.O. Box 1711, Santa Rosa Beach, Florida 32459 or E Mail: DSchu99282@aol.com

BULK ORDER DISCOUNT

Order 15 or more books for a 40% Discount

To order please write:
Preparing The Way Ministries
Steve & Eileen Schultz
P.O. Box 1711
Santa Rosa Beach, FL
32459

BOOKS BY STEVE SCHULTZ

Radical Warriors Require Radical Training

$8.00

Restoration of the Modern-Day Prophet

$6.00

Mentoring and Fathering

$9.00